Recovery

~

By Bedell Phillips

ISBN: 9781958669136

Published by Piscataqua Press
An imprint of RiverRun Bookstore
32 Daniel St., Portsmouth NH 03801
www.ppressbooks.com

Library of Congress Control Number: 2023942708

Printed in the United
States of America

Recovery

~

Bedell Phillips

For Jason, Celeste, Nina, Johnny, Eliot, Torrey, Alice, and Summer
because they bring me joy

Acknowledgements

All gratitude to the literary journals publishing these poems. The author gratefully acknowledges the Best of the Net's nomination for "Thinking about the Violence." Chard deNiord, Tom Sleigh, and Rodney Jones are some but not all of the gifted and patient poets who have guided my work. Deep thanks to my interns, my readers, and my mentor, Tom Lux.

Poet's Notes

Invention of 'Thrums' as a poetic form has driven Bedell's work
in the last several years. Thrums are those threads left on the loom
once a tapestry is removed. They are the poem's last line: the zap,
crux, or its essence. Although Bedell often writes in the thrum format,
she occasionally uses traditional when the poem requires.

Contents

Terrene

I had dinner in the
evening light
on the other side
of the earth
while I slept

an Asian child wakes

Favorite Flower Genera

Kousa Dogwood Purple Lilac Cape Rose
Tradescantia Dandy Man Pink Rhododendron
Yellow Chiffon Calibrachoa Dark Blue Lobelia

summer's thanksgiving

Florida Bounty

Red Ixoras Lacewood Chinese Hibiscus
Moth Orchid Oleander Fire Cracker Bush

Painter's Palette Common Gardenia
Song of India Orange Triumph

Miniature Umbrella Tree Bougainvillea
Light Green Goosefoot

In Plain Sight

atop a honeysuckle tree
fruited with red berries

wobbling but no wind
gray movement

among the leaves
a bird feasts

Dark Gray Day

gray sky waves cresting over water rocks
carry on towards the shore
bubble onto the beach

wide swath of glimmering hope

Nature in Sync

birds come closer to earth
perch on the rooftop
stay near
sing longer
bring comfort

in times of trouble

On the Deck

a young woman and an old woman
sitting on cushioned chairs
chanting the sacred mantra
ah nigh hugh

hallowed sanctuary

Carlin Beach

four of them, 8:30 in the morning kiteboarding
one with an orange sail burst between two waves
another, aqua sail skimming the shoreline
next, green sail with a run at the top of the breakers
last one heading directly out

on the way to London

Infraction

aah aah, I cried
trying to frighten

he didn't budge
looked at me

kept eating
from his small fur hands

again I
shouted

this time he turned
his head

white ruff below his
neck showed

I have no impact
I'm invisible

I need a gun

Recovery

She walked into the beauty parlor, a real stunner
wearing a soft jersey white tunic four whales design

"Wow you're back from the hospital so soon"
"Yup, all that surgery was done in three days"

Sitting next to her husband she had a full on seizure
She fell hard onto her coffee table

They cut back her hair from her forehead four inches deep
they found a brain tumor the size of an orange

"I couldn't believe the prep, they kept asking me questions
do I drink, do I do drugs, four times"

"It's amazing how brave you are, you came through it
fantastic, I'm giving you a new look"

She left with a stunning punk hair cut bald on top, by her ear
half grey half black

Anathemas

Bad weather climate change
Work undone
Mortgage denied
Apartment flooded

Where's my help
Such torment
Such abomination

Such dolor

Dysfunction

a frazzled writer on deadline
finished his book so then
loaded new software but
when he added the latest
version of Word a drop-down
menu froze the computer

his extensive search did not
find the phone number but
Google found it and the call
was answered by a robot

he did a test to ensure
that all the books were
there and would open
but again a drop-down froze
the screen

TMS tech misfunctioning sabotage

Anticipation

Tall middle school kid
went to the YMCA teen dance

That cute girl from English class
with long red curly hair

was standing there with a bunch of her friends
I wanna ask her to dance

What if she says no
I'd be wiped

He started walking and made it all the way over
Shock of the universe she said yes

He didn't realize that she was way tall
It's too late they go out to the dance floor

He asks "is it okay if I put my head on your shoulder?"
She grinning broadly says "why not?"

His nose is by her neck the smell of heaven

Three Mile Hard On

They were on a wilderness island in the middle
of the mountains, no plumbing no electricity.

He walks down the dock a university high diver. He had
known her since he was in Junior High.

Full chested she wore a Tommy Bahama bikini. He got a hard on
right in the middle of everyone on the dock.

Grabbing his old friend he wrestled him to the hard wood
so that no one would see.

Was she turned on?

Three Strikes and You're Out

They were at the Square Grouper right on the inlet. He was tall wearing a beautiful long sleeved blue shirt.

She asked him "have you been married?" He replied "Well it's a story." Not phased she said "Sure."

"Three times" he continued. "First one I was young. My parents liked her. It seemed like what should be done.

Second one was a friend of a friend. She was single and pregnant. We were together for two years. Of course the baby came and it was wonderful.

While in the third marriage I adopted the baby, put my name on the birth certificate with her mother. We were together for 30 years, my third wife and I."

Silent for a bit, she was blown away, startled.

"We're separated," he replied.

"You mean to say you're on the *Find a Love* site and you are not single?"

Silver Internet III

He looked okay on the site
though a thick gray mustache

big dark tall hair on his head, must
be a dye job cuz of the mustache

She got his first message and said

"I was just thinking Exeter is quite
aways away. I didn't realize that.
I don't know if that distance is a
problem or not."

"I travel a lot so distance isn't a
problem for me."

"I thought you like the ocean
but if you don't wanna
come over and the whole
thing is just too far that's fine.
I was interested in talking about where you
work because of all that time I spent
up there in Keene. It's up to you."

"I'll call you and we can talk for a
little bit but I have to leave at one to
talk to my son."

"Sure no problem."

"When we talk again I'll have to tell
you a little bit more about myself. I'm
actually a part-time firefighter for the
Keene Fire Department. I took an
injury to my ankle ten years ago rescuing
a lady and cutting her out of her car.

It's been needing a fuse for about ten
years so I do have a bad right ankle.
Could be a dealbreaker because right
now it's pretty sore. We'll talk more
about it if you're interested."

"Sure let's talk about it when you can.
I am confused will you be available before
dinner? Let me know what works thanks."

"No I am not disabled, my right ankle got
damaged ten years ago in a fire call. I'm a
part-time firefighter for the City of Keene.
Also I'm still with my son so I'm out of
town for the moment but I can connect and
talk with you more about it but if you feel I'm
disabled then I guess I'm no good to you."

"No, you just weren't clear since it had
happened ten years ago but no one has taken
care of you yet. That's why I don't like using
text. I, myself, was on the Appalachian Trail
and was in a cast until just yesterday. Don't
worry about it. We are just getting to know
each other. Yup, call me when you can."

Silver Internet IV

January 14 —
Hello Lucy beautiful picture
What do you do for work?

In the past I had a company
with my ex-husband and now
I am an author and poet

How are you doing today?

January 15 —
I'm in pain I've got tennis elbow
So the texting's not good
Besides I'd like to hear your voice

January 16 —
Good morning Watcha doin'

Working on a story

That's nice can I have your phone number?

January 18 —
(he sent a text at 4am)
I would also like to hear your voice

Hi Never text or call me in the middle
of the night Obviously it interrupts my
sleep Should we continue? Gotta promise
that won't happen ever again

Don't worry

OK I'll take you at your word

January 20 —
OK but since we're both working
let's pick a time to talk What do you think?

I think it's a good idea (he sent right away)

I'm done work for today
Would you like to have a chat
now

Kim Sear

I don't understand

Sorry it was a mistake

January 22 —
Yes I would like us to talk on the phone

Sure let me know what time
you want to do it

January 24 —
OK

January 25 —
Cool to hear from you yesterday
I'm working today

January 26 —
That was the last I heard from him
Ghosted

Silver Internet V

Tall enough with blond, curly hair
A picture of a boat and a swimming pool

His texts were very chatty
Raising hope

Finally the awaited phone call
She liked the sound of his voice

"My wife was horrible
She really went after me."

Wow, he's super disturbed
He hasn't resolved his divorce

"She wasn't just normal bad
She sent me to jail."

Whatever went on
he was impounded

He felt brutality abuse
humiliation and despair

I'm not doing him

Silver Internet VI

Nancy: Your site has confused me Are you living
in Melbourne Australia or are you living in Melbourne
Florida?

Mike: Florida

Nancy: Phew I wonder if you think my town is too far away?

Mike: Not at all

Nancy: That's a good sign we seem to have a lot of conversations

Mike: Lol Still in your pjs?

Nancy: You're making me laugh actually I'm in a long T-shirt
which says relax It was a gift

Mike: Nice

Nancy: Some guys prefer to text as opposed to having an
actual conversation where you hear a person's voice Which do
you prefer?

Mike: Oh I'm in the midst of something But in a little while as soon as
things simmer down here Still a bit excited Lol

Mike: Scare you off? Must have

White Clapboard Village

white village meeting house
painful box pews fear of god pulpit
on high to ensure the impact of his wrath

town antique weathered
framed houses small streets
tall pines glacial climate

they rush inside escape the elements
faces numbed hands chapped
too cold to speak to neighbors

children made to descend
down the basement coal furnace-bucket full
they must dump it outside

back in their home saved   comfort and warmth

Old Age Loneliness

sun setting, reflecting
lavender onto the salt marsh,
spartina grass meandering
along the twisted water

everyone's dancing, not me
hot uncomfortable music
I don't know

can't do those steps
I'm without hope
there's nothing for me

no one cares

Highway to the Lakes Region

in the midst of the city
malls and law offices
stretched on either side of the road

stands of stately white pines
interspersed with glorious elms

sign for Winnipesaukee
Approaching Lakes Region

NH Rt 104 Meredith
ammo store, liquor store, tchotchke stand

she leaves the shore with the beer guzzlers
overflowing trashcans and the violent state of her sacred country

as long as you go back there, it's as wondrous as ever

waiting for the beloved old
open aluminum boat

put her foot on the bow seat
dumped her bag in

when they reached the channel
a giant cabin cruiser cut them off

the wake splashed them
drenched her shirt

long absence but exactly the same

dock, dirt path, new screen door
condom in the black trash can

her postcards put up ten years ago
still unharmed untouched

rough decrepit space houses the bunk bed
below chasmal window cut from old wood wall
water view stretches to the mountains cerulean sky

sanctuary of renewal

Difficulty in Paradise

granite island
deeply forested

sitting on the ladderback chair
searing pain

holding the ice pack
brought by a teenage waiter

college boys in bathing suits half-naked
haul her up to the toilet
look like body builders

she fears they will touch her breasts
he cautiously turns her head leading her inside the bathroom
"be careful I'm going to get you over to the john"

finally down on the dock
they haul her out of the wheelbarrow

shriek of deafening boat sirens
slashes the quiet air

red rescue boat with huge fire hoses mounted on the bow
sharply painted red letters Meredith Water Rescue

the driver says "I'll go slow
so the waves won't smash you"

reached Shep's Boat Landing
but all her possessions still in the hut

the ambulance met them   sirens cleared the way
at the hospital sterile gray floor

she didn't even see a doctor
x-rayed fitted for crutches and a cast

terror and angst but she made it home safe

Our First Space Race

old guys in suits
intrude into
her classroom

the teacher
Mr. Champagne
says "In class today
we are very
lucky…"

everybody wonders
why

"We have special
visitors." If
Mr. Champagne
says so it is
so

the visitors go
to the head of
the class like
she did with her
seeing eye dog
report

"The Russians have
launched a satellite
into outer space.

Our country has lost
it's superiority and we
have lost the space race.

That's why we are here.
We must utilize the next
generation which is you,
to catch us up."

Mr. Champagne said, "This
gentleman is saying
that a group of you
will be chosen to go

down to the college and
will take science classes."

Donnie La Mothe
whispers "This
guy's from outer
space."

She got her first migraine.

Screwed by her Doctor

she felt excruciating pain
went on the computer 8:30 in the morning
found the surgeon's phone number
still at 9:00 no one answered
she hung up tried again

this time loud shrill nah nah nah shriek
kaking-kaking-kak fax noise
the doctor just won't pick up
if I don't get them

I can't leave my home
those ten steps are just too hard
I'm going to lose my job
can't wait on tables

I'm screwed

Significant Rite

A southern governor in speaking
about the Katrina flood shocked her
population by saying "Yes we got the full Monty"

Another southern governor overturned the
abortion rights bill as well as created a law
to allow concealed guns in public

January 6th Insurrection
firebombed the US Capital

Old fart New Hampshire general
told pregnant girls "get over it"

But our rose still blooms

Varanasi's Irony

A British teenager has to leave the tour bus because they are not allowed near the sacred ghats where the bodies are cremated. This town, Varanasi, is a significant Hindu Holy City, famous because if one is cremated there and the ashes are released into the hallowed Ganges River, they will complete reincarnation and they are guaranteed the magnificence of Nirvana.

She must walk down the paved road, edged by beggars and random people urinating on the way down to the Ganges. The smoke rises from fresh ashes as people escape their earthly body.

Above her passage are the famed Digambara monks, who shun all property and wear no clothes. High above her head, dark skinned spread-eagled conspicuous genitals drooping, it's a shocking offense. The terror rose in her like the sacred smoke by the river. She wanted to get out of there. It was foul. But she had come so far to see the sacred cremation.

She kept on going.

World Peril
Call to Action

On March 21, 2023 the United Nations Intergovernmental
Panel on Climate Change announced detailed data showing
our climate is changing. *The New York Times* reported, "A critical
threshold will occur in the next decade. The industrialized nations
will need to make an immediate and drastic shift from fossil fuels
to prevent the planet from overheating dangerously."

This report says that global average temperatures are estimated to
rise 2.7 degrees Fahrenheit above all preindustrial levels, if humans
continue to burn coal, oil and natural gas.

If not addressed severe impacts of catastrophic heatwaves,
flooding, drought, crop failures and species extinction will increase.
Also current straining of food production will deteriorate.

At present record-shattering floods in California and catastrophic
drought in East Africa exist. In addition low lying island nations
and communities that depend on glaciers may face severe fresh
water shortages.

Humanity's actions today will reshape the planet for thousands of years.

Also by Bedell Phillips

POETRY

Edges of Waves
Thrums & Tapestry
Wolf Tail Glimmer
Is There Life
Three Perch Swimming

PROSE

Around the Bend

www.ingramcontent.com/pod-product-compliance
Lightning Source LLC
Chambersburg PA
CBHW022348040426
42449CB00006B/782